The Commoyse

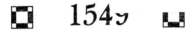

1549

by Nicholas Sotherton

Edited by Susan Yaxley

Drawings by David Yaxley

The Larks Press
Stibbard, Norfolk

First edition of 700 copies printed and published by
the Larks Press
Ordnance Farm House, Guist Bottom, Dereham, Norfolk
June 1987

ISBN 0 948400 04 8

Introduction to the Text

'The Commoyson in Norfolk' was transcribed and edited by Mr Barrett L. Beer in 1976 and printed in the *Journal of Medieval and Renaissance Studies* for that year. This edition is based on the original text, but owes much to his work and is not intended to supersede it, merely to make the text more widely available to those interested in Norfolk's history than it would be in the pages of a learned journal of a decade ago.

The text survives only in a copy of the original made probably in the late sixteenth or early seventeenth century, and is unfortunately incomplete. (B.L. - Harl. MS 1576 fols. 251r to 259r.) It would appear that the version from which the scribe copied was itself damaged and in parts difficult to read. One passage in particular seems to have presented difficulty, as the phrase 'fortasse legendum' (probably to be read) appears several times in the margin. It is thought that the original was written by Nicholas Sotherton within ten years of the events of 1549.

There is some doubt surrounding the identity of Nicholas Sotherton as there were at least two men of that name alive in Norwich at the time. It is fairly certain, however, that he belonged to one of the leading merchant families of Norwich, and he may have been the son of the Nicholas Sotherton who was Mayor of Norwich in 1539, and the brother of the Leonard Sotherton mentioned in the text.

Sotherton writes from the point of view of the rulers of Norwich and shows little sympathy for the rebels, doing his best to belittle their social standing by calling them 'vagabonds and servants' whenever possible. The emphasis of his account is on the dilemma of the city leaders and on the terrorisation of the gentry by the insurgents. He makes no attempt to explain the causes of the trouble. There is no evidence that Sotherton was there himself in 1549, but his account is clearly based on the memories of eye-witnesses such as Austin (Augustine) Steward.

The original spelling has been retained, except that 'v' has been changed to 'u' and 'i' to 'j' where modern usage requires it. Capital letters have been rationalised and some punctuation attempted, though the extraordinary and undisciplined sentence-structure is very difficult to tame. Abbreviations have been expanded and obvious clerical errors removed. The marginal notes, which are omitted from Beer's transcription, have been included in bold type to help the reader to follow the sense of the narrative.

The Commoyson in Norfolk

1549

*The caus of this Rebellion begon in Norffolk by dyvers persons
as the same is reported to bee by divers that uppon enquery did gett
the understanding thereof. Drawne furth by Nicholas Sotherton
with the manner and continuance of the same.*

Upon occasion that by a commandment from the Prince
uppon complaint made for encloseng of divers common
grownds* that divers commissioners upon view thereof by
a day should have done, and for not doeing thereof, was in
A rumor of Norffolk a rumor that in Kent and other places
Assemblies divers that had layd open, perceiving many
others did not the same, and therfore thought good of theyre
owne authority to lay those growneds open allsoe. Which
rumor soe opened and large in talke of dyvers persons as-
cembled att a certen nyht and daie playe in the towne of
At Windham game Hymondham callyd Wyndham game
whieh was there played the Satterday nyght being the vi daie
Anno 1549 Reg of June [July] 1549* and held on the viith
and what di daie and part of the viiith daie being Monday,
which daie the people to depart, and they of Wyndham had

*See notes following the text

3

The first conference some conference to common with
for the Assemblye such as had not cast downe the same;
Robert Ket is motioned emong whome moving the same
to one Robert Kett alias Knight*, whereuppon hee soone
agreeing thereto suffrid some of [those] with him in company to cast downe a certen close of his in Hymondham,
therewith encouragid them that such as would not doe the
like hee wishid theires to bee done in like case, which soe
animated the harts of such of them into whome Rebellion
was easily enterid, that they proceeded further to doe the
The plucking lyke and specially in Flowerdow's close*,
down of closes where the cheife occasion whereof was
gyven, and uppon rebuke therefore of such as were greived
and would have withstand them, they resortinge as to the
sayd Robert as to complaine thereof, the sayde Robert for
lack of Grace, pretending to doe good thereby to the Com-
monwealth, sayd he would assist them with body and goods,
Kett's encoragement whereuppon of a small company att
to the Rebels first not above five or six persons, they encreased to servants and vagabones that they would not be
resysted, and the same Robert with them, after they had
endid theyr purpose att Windham, came forward to Norwich warde to doe the lyke, and uppon Tewsday afternoone
How they proceedid being the ixth daie were come as fur
to Norwich warde as Eaton Wood with in a mile of

4

Norwich, which being hard of by dyvers evyll disposid people in Norwich, there assemblid unto them divers vagrand persons of the sayd Citty of Norwich whoe, partlie uppon former talke att the Game aforesayde, and partly uppon sodeygne admoneshment, were easly assenting to that **Admonicion for** Rebellion. Notwithstanding divers Cyt-**the Common Close** ezins that both misliked of the laying open a close callid the Common Close only tendinge to stow the Neate that the Cytezens used daily to milke for theyr provision, as alsoe that they unlawfully assemblyd to reforme theer owne caus, yeat they procedyd in theyr attempte and after layeinge open that close and other closes thereabout, fearing themselves to haive attempted to [too] farr, by such watchwords as were gyven to them agreid to betake them to some hold or place of force and furthwith assentyd among **How they would assure** themselves to take the Hyll **themselves in Mount Surry** callyd Mount Surry partley for that there uppon in ye place sometime called St Leonards there was a place after the manner of a pylgrymage for resort of people for dyvers diseases, in which place the late Erle of Surrey dysceacid had buildyd a very pleasant, large and goodly place calling it Mount Surreye which, standing up-**The Cituation** pon the brow of an hy hill, had the ryver **of Mount Surrey** beneth yt betwixt the City of Norwich in the West syde thereof, and in the South syde thereof yt

5

hadd a large wood callyd Thorpe Wood and the Towne of Thorpe, and Est and North a goodly Common callyd Mushold, in some places more than six myles over, and beyond the water of the West yt had the Cytty of Norwich, unto the which place and forte for that theyr niest way lay through

Lyscens denyid to passe through ye Cytye the Cytye they cravid lyscens of one Thomas Codd, Mayour, and others his Bretherne and Cyteizins. They had many sharpe and bitter checks for their disorders, and many Comunings were

Meeting of the Cytiezins what to doe had whither it was better to resyst theyr enterprys, or to suffer theyr doings: which for want of warrant therefore from the Prynce, not knowing what might chance, was adjudged a doughtfull enterpryse until further commission from the Prince, which to understand was dyrected their doeing with speed. In the meane season to hast their procedyngs they passed the next

The xth day of June they passed over Helsdone bridge day being the xth daye of June [July] over a lyttyll bridge callyd Helsdon bridge about two myles from Norwich over the ryver with fagots casting into the water, from

How they encamped in Mount Surrey whence, within an hower or somewhat more, they had incamped themselves in the aforesaid Hil toward the wood aforesaid, and presently after gatt the possession of the sayd place callyd Mount Surrey place and there began to determine how to

6

withstand all force against them to bee made; and to have theyr purpose to have a fayre shew and similitude of well **Of theyr holy pretence** doinge, they first procurd a Pryst **in prayer** to mynister theyr morninge and evening prayer in the Inglish tonge, then newly begon to bee frequentyd. **Of their choyse of Captains** Allsoe they would have the **or Governours, Tho. Codd, Mayour,** best men of life and **Tho. Aldrich of Mangrene,** religion to bee their Capteins **Rob. Watson, preacher** emonge whom they chose one Robart Wattson, a preacher in those days of good Estimacon, and Thomas Codd, Mayour of the Cyttye of Norwiche and Thomas Aldrich of Mangrene a two myle from Norwich, a man of good wisdome and honesty and welbelovid; which three persons allthough by no meanis would bee of the Conspiracy, yeat fearing the aforesaid Robert Ket alias Knight, being wickedly led to bee theyr cheife Captaine, might by his wicked determinate advise and cowncell procure such greate inconveniencies by his prepostrous authoritie as ones enterprysed and begone might not easly bee revertyd. The **Why ye persons aforesayd** sayd three nominatid to bee **concented to governe them** with Kett to have the rule and goverment of the said rude people which indeed hapind very well, for that att ech time the said Kett wolde by his sinister will with his adherents command eny unlawfull things to bee done in the contry, the seid Thomas Aldrich did let

How they did [prevent] and pacifie the controversies
pacifie Evils therein. And allsoe the sayd Ket etc. willed
the like doing in Norwich, that did Thomas Codd lett, and
in that they together agreid not in, that did Robert Watson
the preacher by his perswasion lett; nott withstanding as the
The confusid order head Kett soe were the people con-
of Kett's Commissioners fuzid in commanding precepts
and how they did to attach Gentellmen prisoners, others
to provide viand for theyr returne, that is bred corne and
drinke, some to bee baken and brued, others to go in Com-
mysson to lay open common growndes, others to encrease
theyr members, in which inordinate thinge the seid Mr Codd,
Mr Aldrich and the seid Mr Wattson were partley faine to
agree lest, they being out of favour and place, others might
Why the Capteins come to bring all things out of frame
aforesayd discemblyd in that now might partly bee well
some things framid. And the rather they assentid to know
the people in better order during answer from the Prynce
what ells they might furder doe. Notwithstanding during
By what means the fame of this unlawfull assemblie for
ye Rebels encreased that in Suffolk, Kent and other placis
the Commons attempted the lyke enterpryse, soe that in the
And why they were not Realme was up to a greate num-
att ye first supprysed ber hard to suppryse which was the
lenger or any answer came; in the which tyme were gatherid

to this Company in Norfolk by report and judgment to the number of xx thousand persons* in the space of iij or iiij weekes which soe continued untill vj weekes which was Magdalyn Even; in the meane tyme Kett and his Company ceasid not to assure themselvis. And first they went to old Paston Hall and gett ordinance from thence and soe to Yermoth and other placis and brought in forsan severall peeces **Theyr preparation for** one and another, and came into **Ordinance and Munition** Norwich and sent to Lynne and other placis and what theye could gett that were sent, they browt with them both shott, powder, ammunicion, corne, cattell, mony and every thing ells, and browt the gretest part to the Rebellis Campe and some they convertid to their private use. Whylst theis things were a complaining of to the Governours aforeseyde they appoynted a place of ascemblye **Of their Tre of Reformacion** emonge them in an oken **to hear & determine causes** tre in that place which they bordid to stand on, uppon which tre at ye first did none come but Kett and the rest of the Governours* where the people oute of were admonishid to beware of their robbinge, spoy- **How little they regardid** linge and other theyr evil de- **to bee admonished** meanors and what accompte they had to make, but that lyttil prevailid for they cryid out of the **Cause they ragid** Gentlemen as well for that they would **of Gentlemen** not pull down theyr enclosid growndis, as

9

allsoe understood they by letters fownd emonge theyr sarvants how they sowt by all weyes to suppres them, and
whatsoever was sayde they would downe with them soe that

Of theyr pursuit within a ij or iij weekes they had so pur-
of Gentlemen suyd the Gentlemen from all parts that in
noe place durst one Gentleman keepe his house, but were
faine to spoile themselves of theyr apparrell and lye and keepe
How Gentlemen in woods and lownde [secluded] placis
were faine to doe where noe resorte was; and some fledd
owte of the contrye and gladd they were in theyr howses
for saving of the rest of theyr goods and catell to provide for
them daiely bred, mete, drinke and all other viands and to
carry the same at their charge even home to the Rebellis
Campe, and that for the savinge theyr wyves and chydren
and sarvants. Notwithstanding were dyvers Gentlemen taken
How Gentlemen were and browt to prison, some in Nor-
used and prisoned wich prison, and some on Norwich
Castle and some in Surrey Place. And whylst they wantid
How they did in ye Cytie money they compellid the
for theyr tresury and Mayour such money as was in the
munition and ye Cytezins threasure of ye Cytie to bee
at commandment att theyr commandment which was
faine to bee granted unto exepte upon private warning the
same was otherwyse conveied awaye. All other municion
they gatt by force owt of the Cytie and commanded every

Citezin to bee to them assistent, setting their face to bee the King's friends and to defend the King's Laws soe impudent were they now become; yea, now they would noe more bee advertizid by their Governours, but theyr Governours must concent to them and by this farr had they not only all Gentyllmen & yeomen att theyr commandment, but for the most of estimacion in ye Cyttie; whereuppon dyvers of the best

How ye Cytezins were Cytezins with theyr wyves, chil-
faine to depart and dren were faine to depart the Cyttye
spare up theyr occupiengs for that they would by noe meanis obey them, and spare up [shut up] their occupyeng & otheyr theyr substance in secret wyse; which understandid from thence furth were accompid of the rebellis as Traytors and they in the Campe made Havock of all they could gett,

What Havock and cutt downe all the wood of the place to
ye Rebellis make roste and make greate fiers therein both night and daye when the state of the Cyttie begon to bee in

The Misere of most mysserable case that all men looked
the Cyttie for utter destruction both of lyfe and goods.
Then the remnant that fearid God, seing the plage thus of

How they being sorrowful sorrowe encreasing, fell to
fell to prayer prayer and holye lyffe and wishid but to see the day that after they might talke thereof, looking never to recover helpe againe nor to see theyr Cyttie ageine to prosper, and the Rebellis for their [part] did thrett to fyer the

11

The Rebellis thrett Cyttie and to consume the substance
to fyer the Cyttie and fainely if in everi pointe they assentid not to them. Besides, to call the people with, they made
How they made Larums Larums that Gentlemen were
by ringing Bells & to comming against them by ringing
enlarge their Companye of Bells and fireing of Beacons,
by which meanis resortid greate numbers of people and provision owte of all Towns in Norfolke, Suffolke and dyvers
others placis and shyres in Ingland*; and in the way of theyr
How they robbid pastures parte, and such as had Kett's
myddows and houses Commission on the other parte,
take owte of closes, pastures, and Myddows and owte of
men's houses all manner of horses, and of grett Cattle iij M
and more, and of sheep xx M and more, an deere oute of
dyvers parks in greate numbre besides swans, geese, and all
What good peny other foulis paying nothing therefore
worthe they sold and sold mutton for jd a quarter veri
good*, and theis they browte to their Campe which they
callid the greate Campe of Mushold; and the Gentyllmen
How they handled Gent. they tooke they browte to the
browte to them and how Tree of Reformacion to bee
their voices prevailid seene of the people to demande
what they would doe with them: where some cryde "Hang
him!" and some "Kill him!", and some that heard noe word
cryd even as the rest even when themselvis, being demandid

12

why they criyd, answerd for that theyr fellows afore did the like, and indeede they did presse theyr weapons to kyll some of those Gentyllmen browte to them which they did of such **How Mr Wharton** malice that one Mr Wharton, being **emong them was nye slaine** garded with a lane of men on both sydes from the said tre into the Cyttie, they pricked him with theyr spearis and other weapons on purpose to kill him had they not had greate helpe to withstand theer malice and creweltye; and further the rest of the Gentyllmenne imprisoned they fettrid with chenis and locks and pointid divers to ward them for escapinge. And in the meane tyme, with Kett's authority, both constables and other officers enforcid with theyr Company to keepe the Gates that the Cytezins shuld not soe fast range forth the Cyttie as allsoe that noe Gentyllmenne shuld escape.*

How one Leonard Sotherton Whilst thus they had con-
was examinid att ye Corte tinuid about a v weekes & in
of theyr dimeanour all this ceason came noe command-
& cravid pardon & what a ment from the Prynce to the
Harrold offrid them then Cytezins and that about that
when hee was sent therfore tyme one Leonard Sotherton,
a Cytezin of Norwich, had occasion to goe to London uppon cheife occasion to avoid ye Cyttie for his owne savegard as others did the same, callyd before ye Counsill to declare the truth of the sayde rebellion's estate whereof hee made reporte

according to his knowledge, and after hee had cravid pardon
and besought the King's Majestie's Grace for pardon to be
offrid unto theis Rebellis, hoping that the office thereof
would both glad a greate numbre of harts that would have
remorse of theyr rebellion, and to cause the same to revarte
and returne to theyr habitations as faithfull and true subjects
are to doe; which sayd Leonard Sotherton was commanded
to waite uppon one of the King's Grace's Harrold att armis
named Yorke, which hastely returned home and by the xxi
day of July, then the even of Mare Magdalen, about noone
entred the Cyttie where furthwith the sayd Yorke in his
cote armour in the whole assemblye of people did reade and
declare the King's most gracious pardon to all that wolde
humblee submit themselvis and depart quietly every man to
his howse to enjoy the benefit thereof; whereupon a greate
How many received numbre on theyr knees fell downe
the pardon thankfully giving God and the King's Maj-
estye greate thanks for his Gracis clemenci and pitti. Not-
Ket withstandeth pardon withstanding the wretched man
encourageth other Kett refuzid the same and seid openly
to take his part hee had not offended* nor deserved the
King's pardon and soe requird as many as would try and
abyde with him to take his parte and remaine still, where-
The Harrold defy him uppon the most numbre remained.
and all that take his part Then the Harrold in the King's

14

name defyde him and called him Traytour with all that tooke

The Cytizens betake his part and therewith the Harrold
themselves to the Cyttie departing into the Cyttie with a
and to defend ye Rebellis greate numbre that received the
pardon together with the sayd Thomas Codd, Mayour, and
Thomas Aldrich, before Governors as beforsayd with Kett
of their rude and rusticall people, and furthwith did shut the
Citty gates. After the sayd gates [were] rampeird & shut the
sayd Mayour furthwith deliverd out of prison all such Gentyllemen as the sayd Kett had before shit up as well in the
Guyld Hall as the Castle to meete together to peruse and to
doe that might in theyr knoledge bee best to save the Cyttie
and defend [repel] the Rebellis and keepe them from victual;
which soone after they perceived that through ye falshood
of many of theyr Cyttizins the seid Rebels were entrid. But
seing the Rebels entrid*, feine was the seid Mayour to com-
mitte them againe to pryson for theyr saveguard lest for
theyr delivery the Cittye should feare the worse; whereupon
they were shut up agen.

How the Cyttie shot This done they made with all ex-
theyr Ordinance & pedition the Ordenance of the Cyttie,
defended ye Cyttie & being vj small peeces, to be levelid
wardid ye decade places to them out the place callid the
Castle ditches to ward them & the night drawing on the seid
Thomas Codd with thadvise of his brethren the Aldermen

15

and others of the Cytezins causid good watch & ward to bee
kept in especial att the dangerousest places; in the which
places dyd watch in theyr harneis a certeyne of both Aldermen and Commoners with theyr sarvants att every gate and
circuyte of walls with the adyce of those Gentyllemen that
afore were prysoners, and the rest rydde about from place
to place to belaye [invest] that nether enterance or assawlte
or larum shuld bee made, but wyth as much dyligence and
connynge as they could dyd endeavor themselvis to both
keepe out the Rebellis and dispoyle them of victualls, and
pretendyng to continue the same untyll some good hope of
recovery or helpe by the Prynce's power shuld come. And
How ye Ordenance was to make all sure in the nyght the
remooved to ye water's side Ordenaunce of the Cyttie
to them ward & was placed alongst the ryver with good
what the Rebellis did guard of men in the Hospitall Myd-
dowes for that it was the weakest place, and as they of the
Cyttie shott att them, they did the lyke into the Cyttie all
nyght and the Rebellis perceiving in the morninge that theyr
shott went over the Cyttye they browte downe theyr Ordenaunce from the lower part of the Hyll, but fearing to remaine there for that the Cyttie shot drive them of [off],
whereuppon theyr Ordenaunce did small hurt.
Kett's message to the Cyttie Thus the day appearing on
to bee possessed as before Monday the xxiiijth daie of

16

or ells they would enter   June [July] the seide Kett sent
the Cyttie by force   downe one James Williams of Norwich, Taylor, with a banner of truce in messuage unto Mr Mayour with allsoe one Ralph Sutton of Norwich, Hattrer, that if the Mayour would suffer them to enjoy the Cyttie as to make their provision as they had done before or ells they would enter the Cyttie by force, whoe was answerid that neither to cum or have nourishment of the Cyttie shuld bee grantyd but defyans utterly as Traytours. And whylst there was provision making within the Cyttie to wythstand them every waye & that with Bowmen, as they came from the
Of the Skirmish and   Hyll they were shott att wyth gret
ye Rebellis impudency   numbre of arrowes, soe impudent were they and soe desperate that of theyr vagabond boyes [wyth reverens spoken] brychles and bearars syde came emong the thickett of the arrows and gathred them up when some of the seid arrows stack fast in theyr leggs and other parts and did therwith most shamefully turne up theyr bare tayles agenst those which did shoote, whych soe dysmayed the Archers that it tooke theyr hart from them. Besydes for
Whereuppon they entred   want of powder the shott fol-
the Cyttie through the ryver   lowed not, neyther were
and dryve the Cytezins backe   the Gonnars perfyt in the
& soe had possession of ye Cyttie   Cyttie to order theyr peeces, which the Rebellis perceivinge well, and when they

17

dyscernyd from the Hyll that many of the Cytezins were departid from the straight and other placis of the wallis where another part of the Rebellys made assawlt, and that many other Cytizins were some in theyr howses about theyr businesse, even then about xi or xij of the clocke att noone the seid raggyd boyes and desperate vagabons in greate numbre wyth halbers, spers, swerds, and other weapons, and some wyth muck forks, pytch forks etc. hastely came runnyng downe the Hyll and tooke the ryver most desperately mervelous to the beholders, as soe suddenly abashid them that the Gonnar fearid to shote. There was soe greate a numbre about him that hee left his Ordenaunce and fledd, and the rest that watchid, seing themselvis nothing to resist, allsoe hastily departid when the Rebellis soe followid that happy was hee that could take howse. And theis soe entrid through **The Citty Ordenaunce** the ryver, on [one] part of them **carryed to ye Campe and** unrampired the gates and car-**how they used the Cytezins** ryed the vj peeces of Ordinance to the Hylles with the instruments thereto, and the other parte came furthe into the Cyttie and by the way called the Cytezins Traytours etc. that few or none durst looke out theyr haste was so suddeigne uppon them. Whilst theis **The Harrold agen** things was a doing and beholden of ye **offrid them pardon** Harward att armis, and hee, for that **which they refuzid** his commission serve for two daies, went himself emong them and offryd ageyne unto the King's pardon which they utterly refuzid and cryed & howlyd and showtyd as they had wonne theyr purpose even the wholle way as they went to the Crosse of the market* to the greate admiration of the Harrold and of all the Cyttie. And the

The Harrold desier Harrold accompanied with Austin
and is browte out of Styward Alderman and others, seing
the Cyttie and departs theyr rudenes & partly fearing
theyr desperatenes, desyred the seid Mr Styward to bring him out of the Cyttie, which after hee was brought furth St. Stephen's gate departed straight to the Corte, the Cyttie with the Rebellis being in greate rowre which still went

The Rebellis seeke howling abroade the Cittye and calld
to bee revenged of for the seid Leonard Sotherton mean-
Leonard Sotherton for ing to him and his to doe some
getting theyr pardon mischeefe for that hee was one that browte downe the pardon in soe much that both Leonard and his brethren* from thencefurth durst noe more to bee seene abroad.

Kett apprehend Th. Codd Then the seid wretched Kett
Th. Aldrich, Ro. Watson by force made the seid Thomas
& other Aldermen and put Codd, Mayour, and Thomas
some of them in chaines & fetters Aldrich aforesayd & Robert Watson to bee apprehendid in the Cyttie. Soe did they one William Rogers, Alderman, John Himerstone,

Alderman, William Brampton Gent.* and divers others of worshippe whome they carryed prisoners to theyr Campe and putt them in hold in Surrey Place, where they remayned in chaines & fetters unto the last daye that some by God's provision was savid and some dyed.

A new encrease Whylst theis things were a doing in the **of the Campe** Cyttie, Kett did send abroade* by his Embassators to rayse the whole Country, by which means resortid to him a greate numbre and allthough the seid Thomas **The Mayour &** Codd and Thomas Aldrich were taken **Thomas Aldrich pardond** prysoners and of themselvis att greate defiance with Kett, yeat partly for that the Cytezins would not have the Mayour in prison and for the good modesty of Thomas Aldrich for which hee was beloved of Cyttie and Countrye for which, notwithstanding Kett, they wold bee ordered by, for the which, though they allways protested Kett to bee a Traytor & his, yeat was Kett allways **How Kett was feine to** feine to allow them in such order **suffer & grant ye Mayour** as they would and att theyr **liberty to goe & come** hands did the seid Kett suffer manasses and threts soe pleasid God to putt into the people's mynds and soe cam that well to passe, for much determination was thereby lettyd and soe had the Mayour many tymes liberty to goe and cum into the Cyttie by whose advice prudently was as many evils foreseene as might bee.

The Mayour for ye most part Notwithstanding for that
was feine to bee in ye Camp the seid Mayour was faine
& therefore appoynted for the most part to bee att the
Mr Styward deputy that Camp to see the best ordre there,
ordred ye Cytizins well hee appoynted Mr Awsten Styward, Alderman, to bee his depute in the Cyttie whoe very
wisely uppon advice did allways foresee evylls and, for that
hee had allways bin a good and modest man, hee was beloved of poore and rich and att this well contentid of many
to bee obeyid & hee wyth Mr Harry Batto, Alderman, and
John Atkins, Shreives, wyth other theyr assistence kept the
Cytezins, except the most vagrand and vacabond persons, in
good quiet.

Kett calleth the prisoners During this tyme dyd Kett use
before him to bee examined dayly to call the Gentlemen
prisoners before him into the tre called the Tre of Reformacion which was not done wythout the whole multitude,
The Gent. ordrid and them they had noe complaints of
as ye people would they cryd 'A good man, a good man!'
the other that were complaind of they cryid 'Hang him, hang
him!' wythout furder judgement yea though the seid Gentlemen by eny ways made to them intercession and promysd
them amendment soe maliciously were they bent.

And after xiiij or xvj daies it pleased the King's Majesty
to send downe to Norwich to represse theis Rebellis ye Lord

21

The coming of ye   Marquis of Northampton* wyth the
Lord Marquis and others   Lord Sheffeyld, the old Lord
to vanquish theis Rebellis wyth men   Waydsworth* and
others number of Knights as Sir Anthony Denny, Sir Ralph
Sadler, Sir Richard a Lee, Sir Richard Southwell and dyvers
other Knights, Squyers an Gentyllmen and dyvers Italians,
strangers and others to the number of xij or xiijC persons as
was seid, and after the Lord Marquesse, Leiuetenant to the
King's Majesty, being wythin a Myle of the Cyttie, and by a
The Cyttie summon'd   Harrole of Armis callyd Norrice
to receive ye Lord Marquis   had summoned the Cyttie,
whereuppon the seid Awsten Styward, depute for the Mayour, had understand the Lord Leiuetenant's pleasure to bee
recevid into the Cyttie wyth his power according to there
dutes the seid Awsten being in person att the seid gates of
St. Steven hastely gave notice thereof to the Mayour, then
wyth Kett in the Camp whoe by noe meanis would suffer
the seid Mayour from him to depart but kept hym perforce,
The Mayour could not bee   whereuppon the seid Mayour
suffrid to receive the   requirid ye seid deputy to take the
Lord Marquis   sword and meete wyth his Honor and show
the cause of the Mayour's absens, whych the seid deputy did
The depute wyth the swerd   and after he had kyssid the
meetith hym   the swerd and delyverid it to his Honor, the
seid swerd hee delyverid to Sir Richard Sothwell whoe bare

22

it before him bare-headed, wherewyth hee entrid wyth his **The Lord Marquis enter** power the Cyttie att the gate **the Cyttie & come into** aforesayde and came soe into the **the Council Chamber &** Markett and to the Guyld Hall **was refreshid with others** of the same Cyttie and in the Councell Chamber refreshyd him and drank a cup of wine wyth other his assystance there taking order for keeping watch etc.

The Lord Marquis After which done his Honor repayrid **lodgeth att the deputies** to the howse of the seid deputy, where hee with the Lords, Knights and Gentilmen suppyd, in whose gallery rested in theyre armore uppon cushions and pillows divers Italians and wher that daye towards night one of the seid Italians called Cheavers, a Gentillman, in skirmish with them was taken of the Rebellis gorgeously apparrelled & carryed up to the Campe, the seyd Rebellis not content to **A Gent. of the Lord Marquis** hold him prysoner but for **taken in skirmish** his apparell sake was hanged over the **hanged of the Rebellis** walls by a wretched Rebell, one Cayme of Bongege [Bungay] allthough there would have bin given a C li for his life, notwithstanding hee had the like reward within a month after.

How they gardid the Cyttie Notwithstanding the Lords **& what they did** & Nobilities savety the rest of the souldiours were appoynted to guard the Cyttie in every part

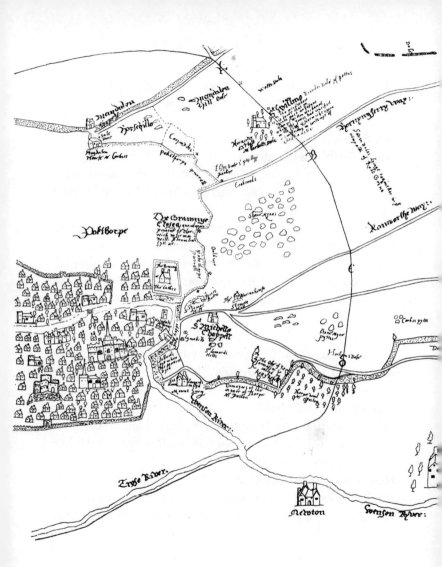

Mandeleu Chapell

Magdalen Hill Odar

Horschillo

Magdalen Mouke ni Corbett

Pokethorpe grounde

Capro ditch

Willing

Harrolds Hill ni Corbetts Dale

t' Hy clock's pytt styp parker

Crosrode

The Gramye Close agrouudeso proceedeso Edward wich n' ye me priell' a hundred Hill di'

Dobsthorpe

Stone waas

Pokethorpe grounde

Oullors

The grene

The luther

S' James Gate

The Warrenhouse The grene

St Michelle Chappell

St Edwards Hills

Gynwells

Edwards Gate ni Adam

Mount Surry

The oke of ye Reformacon called K Ketts oke

Domayneo of the mano' of M' Paston

Harpoarodanni ye Gallen

Stone Laync Pyttes

Colcappe

Mownt Surry

Harpoarodanni ye Gallen

Thorpen Riuer:

Trese Riuer:

Neuton

Wenson Riuer:

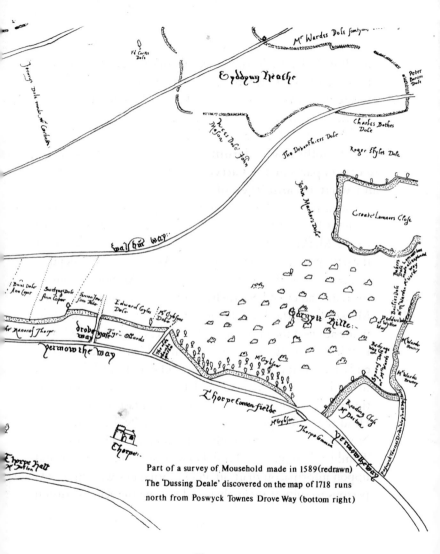

Part of a survey of Mousehold made in 1589(redrawn)
The 'Dussing Deale' discovered on the map of 1718 runs
north from Poswyck Townes Drove Way (bottom right)

needful all that night and especially in the Markyt place was the cheefe nombre where were made bonfires and lights and whereunto divers noblemen and officers attendid & where Sir Edward Ward was the Knight Marshall and gave the watchword, and when att midnight that each one attendid **The Rebellis made alarum** uppon his office the Rebellis **in divers parts of the Cittye** made alarum in divers parts **and what became thereof** of the Cittye whereon after the seyd Knight Marshall had reysid up the Lord Leiutenant with his Lords, Knights and others they in half armour went to the Markitt where the whole power was in rydenes till the day spring,* where the seid Mr Austen Steward, depute, was sent to the old Lord Weinford, to Sir Anthony Dennye, Sir Rafe Sadler and Sir Richard a Lee sitting in a stall of the Market from the Lord Leiuetenant and the Lord Sheffyld whoe advysid the rampering up of divers placis for the better keeping the Citty with fewer men; which was done presently by the appoyntment of the seid depute with labourers toward the water syde, which labourers after they had continued till viij of the clock and after breakfast att the Maydes Head the seid deputy following the seid worke and seeing Norrice, the Harrold, with a Trumpetter riding through Tombland uppon the Lord Leiutenant's comandment and uppon informacon thatt att Pockthorp gates was iiij or v C persons to submit themselves and receive the King's pardon which he was gon to offer them itt; att which though the seid deputy was glad and for joy went with them to the corner tower att Pockthorpe where was Sir John Clere and in another tower Sir Thomas Paston and others, was found to bee neither man, woman nor childe to appere. Notwithstanding the Harrold soundid his

At ye sound of the trumpet by ye Harrold what hapnid trumpet att which came gallopping downe one John Floateman of Beccles and under the seid tower the Harrold after hee had bid him stand and feare not and askyd if hee would declare to his Companye that uppon theyr submyssion the should have pardon, att which tyme came to him from the Campe a xx ty persons more, in whose presence the seid Floateman answrid hee defyde the Lord Leiuetenant and seid he was a Traytour nor wulde of

The obstinacy of the Rebellis & of the entre his pardon, nor had deservid pardon, but that they were the King's true subjects in the which whyle was browte word that the Rebellis had entrid the Cyttie neere the Hospitall. To which place over the Whyte Friars bridge the Harrold rode and the seid deputy rode another way into Tombelond to see what would cum of ytt, and in the playne before the Pallace gate of the Bishop the Lord Leiuetenant's souldiours fought with

A skirmish where 40 persons were slayne the Rebellis where was slayne above forty persons* furthwith and many of the Lord Leiuetenant's men departid sore hurt, in

The Lord Sheffyld slaine   whych conflict was the Lord
where at Rebellis rejoycid   Sheffyld slaine about the Hos-
pital corner by founding his horse in a dyke, to which place
were the Lord's launce souldiours harted forwards, att whose
deth the Lord shewid what hee was though that prevailed
not, and att whose deth they made greate joy and one Fulk
with others contendid to whome the prayse was worthie
whose reward was noe more shortlye after but they hangid
save the neck in the Tree of Reformacon; uppon the which
The Rebellis enter soe fast   Lord's deth approached soe
that the Lord Marquis powre   many Rebellis as the rest of
fleeth & departith the Cyttie   the Lord's launc power fled
with divers Cytezins &   to ye Markit to theire Lord, and
servants & how every   seeing them not hable to resist, the
man shift for himself   seide Lords departed the Cyttie with
his power with whome departid divers Cytezins and men's
servants ageine to London ward, and that by certen men's
houses of worshippe from which howses every man made
away that they had both plate, mony, and stuffe, and the
Cytezins did the like, some in wells, some in ponds and other
secret places the same did hide that it might not bee helping
to the Rebellis thereafter. In the which conflicte there departid with them many that had wives and children, some
that were with childe, some that were sicke and deseasid,
which were fayne to leave them all, and some fled in theyr

doublets and hosen and some in there lightest garments beste to escape & make haste away and allsoe leaving theyr substance & other commodities.

Of the amase Whyll these things were a doing and the
of ye deputye seid Mr Steward, debute, dowghtfull what to doe and entring his howse & finding his servants departed wyth the Armie of the Lord Leiuetenant that returnid till the Lord Warwick's cominge, and seeing the Citty empty of all assistance & every man's doore shutt and that wyth haste one of the Lord Leiftenant's servants wyth his horse were delyvered a payre of silver flaggons and gon, and now comfortlesse, alone beholding out of his highest gallery that the
The Rebellis set Holm Streete Rebellis had set ye whole
on fire & alsoe 5 of ye Cyttie howses in the streete callyd
gates & a Company of Rebellis Holmstreete afyer on
came to ye Deputie's howse & both sydes with a greett
violently used him & cald him part of the Hospitall
Traytour & serchid his howse howses of office that longid
for Gentlemen to bee rid after to ye poore in that howse
under pretence came another and allsoe the Cyttie gates
Company that brake open his called Bishop's gates with
shop & carried that there was the leade thereof molten and the gates & howses of them of Pockthorp, Magdaline, St. Austen's, Costney and Bestret gates all on fier that daie* & that in the feilds without was coming with a drum before

29

them in att St. Austen's gates a greate numbre of Rebellis
that att the gate of the seid debute rappid & cryde 'Set fire
in the gates!' etc. att which the seid debute required an old
man that kept the gate to open the klyckett when they came
thrusting in & violently fell on the seid debute to plucke his
cloake from him and callid him Traytor asking for the Lord
Marquis and others that there were lodged, which awns-
wered they were departid. Notwithstanding after they had
cerched every hole & place and found none to qualify their
feircenes, hee was faine to give them the wholl mony in his
purse to departe, after whose departure came another Company that brake open his shop & in burthens carryed all that
their was tyll one Doo of theyr Company, a servant of Mr
Smith of Huntingfeilds, had sharply told them for robbing
and spoyling they all should bee hangid whereuppon many
of theyr fardles were cast agen into the shopp; whome to
ridde was fayne to bee cutt both shirt cloaths & doublet cloths
of fustian & given them to save ye rest. And after theyr de-

Another Company come to doe parture came another
ye like & soe they did in Company to have spoyled had
every howse they came to not the seid Doo & three or
foure mor kept them of saying hee was spoyled before. And
as the seid Rebellis served the seid debute soe, under pretens
of seeking for Gentlemen, they entrid every man's howse
and spoylid all they could come by in so much that, thowgh

30

the most parte of the best of the Cyttie were departid as is **How servants did to** aforesayde, yeat the servants of the **save theyr Mrs goods** seid Cytezins to save ye rest of theyr Masters' goods devisid to bake bred & to rost, bake pasties & give it unto them to save the rest notwythstanding greate losses ensuid to many.

The Rebellis have ye Cittye And now began the Rebellis **at theyr comandment** againe to possess the Cittye and to have Aldermen and Constables att their commandments and in tyme of raine in the night season they incampid in the Cathedral church callyd Christ's Church in Norwich & had the rewle to doe what them listed and kept the gates themselves of the Cittye wyth the prisens & other placis soe that they rewled the wholle & would command men by howses to watch theyr Campe & gates in the night which both many men and theyr servants then att home were feine to doe untill God after gave them victory.

The Rebellis by preachers In the meane whyle the Deb- **were taught & warned** ute and others procured Dr Barret, a preacher, and other preachers to goe up among them & preach God word. Which notwithstanding helpid not att all, for soe impudent were they & out of ordre, and soe continued tyll the Lord of Warwicke was coming downe with an Armye when that they understood they preparid themselves to withstande.

The Cyttie void of all help Whilst now there was no
their goods wallid up hope that any Cytezin looked for
for fere of burning to enjoy his owne: such as had trusty
servants causid theyr goods, bonds, stuffe and mony to bee
made up in wallis & sellers for that they looked with fire to
bee consumed, but the Masters themselvis in many places
Men parrid in romis was feine to bee parrid up in romis
& lowne placis & other secret placis lest if they had bin
taken prisoners as other Gentylmen were, they shuld bee
dryven to rebell.

Whylst theis things were a doeing and that the King was
advertisid of theyr doeings that by noe meanis they would
avert from theyer rebellion, and that noe pardon would bee
receivid, the King sent into Lincolnshire and other placis of
the Realme and mustridd and toke up a greate numbre of
souldiours and allsoe sent for divers Launce Knights and
other strangers to make a power to suppres the seide Rebells
all which, appareld & in readines had the Lord Warwicke
appoynted Lord Leiuetenant of ye Army, came furthward
from London & by Newmarket & soe to Norwich ward
with all expedicion they might.

The Lord Warwicke approchith The xiij of August and
with his Company Barthylmewe Even* the seide Lord of
viewd & bene 12,000 Warwicke, Leiuetenant of the King's
approching to the Cyttie and within a mile lay abrode with

his army which out of steeples and towers was vewed soe that Kett himself came thereto; which Leiutenant was accompanid with the Lord Marquis that had bin their before, the Lord Willoughby, the Lord Powes, the Lord Bray with grett nombre of Lords, Knights and Squiers and Gentylmen & others with gret store of armour, munycon, shot, powdre, ordynance shott, whose nombre is written to bee xij M which ye night before had lyen att Intwood at Sir Thomas Gresham's place a ij miles of. The seid Lord of his clemencie and for avoiding of bloudshed & saving the Gentylmen in captivity sent his Harrold Norrice to summon the Cyttie to open the gates for his entrye, which Kett hering requirid Awsten Steward & Robert Rugge, Aldermen, to know his embassaye which seide was to know if they would receive in the Leif-**The Aldermen** tenant. The seid Aldermen, lett out at a **request for pardon** posterne, answered that they had rather then a greate summe of mony they might bee lett in and seid they rather thought the seide Harrold was to come to offer pardon to them that would receive it, whereuppon after a pawse till the Harrold had spoken with the Lord Leiuetenant whoe after one quarter of an hower saide, soe the parcullis were pullid up, hee would see what to doe; which after the entrance came a xxx or xl of the Rebellis well horsid that rid in couples before the Harrold, the Trumpetter and two Aldermen through ye Cittee to ye gate next the Rebellis

The Harrold entry whom   Campe where after ye sound
ye Rebellis accompanith   of ye trumpett and a gret num-
through ye Cittie to ye   bre assemblyd to the Hylles syde
Camp & what they doe   and that ye seide Horsmen re-
questid and went to warne them to stand all arraye that re-
maynid, which as they did whylst the Harrold, Trumpetter
& two Aldermen passid through them they put of theyr caps
& cryed "God save King Edward!" whome after the Harrold
commended therfor and the Aldermen desired to keepe theyr
arraye & they passid through ye ranks quietly the space of a
quarter of a myle & had steid uppon a Hyll neere the Campe*
tyll Kett came with a greate nombre about to here, the seid
Harrold seid the King's Majestie hath sent downe the Earle
of Warwick, his Highnes' Leiuetenant with his Majestie's
power, to suppres those Rebellis, but of his clemency and
pitty had of ye destruction of his naturall people sent word
that if they would, like naturall subjects, repent of theyr demeanour and humbly submit themselvis to ye King's mercy
hee would graunt to them his Highnes' pardon for life and
The pardon is granted   goods, Kett only excepted, if not
them or els ye sword   hee protestid, wyth His helpe in
whome his confidence rested, hee would never depart out of
the place till without pitty & mercy hee had vanquisht them
The frayality of some   with the sword. Whereuppon a
& obstinacy of ye rest   grett nombre in feare tremblid,

34

others seide it was but faire words till they were discevered and then to bee hangid up, others seid hee was not sent by ye Kinge, nor was his Harrold, but made by the Gentilmen putting on him a peice of an old Cope for his cote armour, with other despightfull words etc. After which ye Harrold and Kett rode together through the ranks & steid in another place to doe the same. Before the end thereof, for that an ungracious ladd on the other syde had turnid his tayle to them above that one with a corrier shot att him & slew him wherewith came riding through the wood a xij or more horsmen exclaiming that the Harrold cam not but for a traine to have them all destroyid, saying, "Our men are kylled by the water syde, whereat they severed them like mad men". Yeat the Harrold & Kett rode through the rage without staye to a place callyd Sturthyll where half way downe Kett, willing to have gon with the Harrold to the Lord Leiuetenant, was followed with the Company saying, "Whither away? Whither away, Mr Kett? If you goe, wee will goe with you, and with you will live and dye." The Harrold, perceiving a greate numbre following, required Kett to goe backe againe to pacifie them; which

Kett & ye Harrold ride together

A Tumult risen among them whereat ye Harrold for feare departid & Kett rid with him to steere him wher Kett would have gon with him but the Rebellis would not

The Harrold pray him to depart

with his Company returnid to Mushold and the Harrold,
Trumpetter & Aldermen hastid to ye Lord Leiftenant to in-
forme him of theyr doings and soe the Rebellis held him out

Ordinance preparid   whereat the seid Lord Leiftenant cau-
to the gates   sid the Master of the Ordenance to breake open
the gates.   Whyle which was a furnishinge the Lord Leiftenant, resolvid by Mr Steward, Alderman, of a posterne
The pisoners breake in   called Brazen gate being ramperd,
att the Brazen gate   causid his pyoneers to breake it open
where the souldiours first entrid & drive back ye Rebellis
The Ordinance dischargid   where the Master of the Ordinance dischargid and brake ye halfe gate & percullis where
Captain Drury   the seid Lord Marquis with Captaine Drury
skore ye streets   and his band entrid and skorid the streets
& killed divers Rebellis. In the meane tyme the seid Austin
Steward causid Westwick gate to bee sett open, where the
The Lord Warwick   Lord Leiftenant with all his Armye
with his Army enter   cam quietly in through that high
the Westwick gate   streete into the Markett where divers
Rebellis were fownd and hangid that night and to the which
place came the whole Cytezins with their servants that had
long bin hid, as is aforesayd, and cryde for pardon, to whome
the Lord Leiutenant answrid they should have pardon and
commandid every man home to his howse and keepe the
same that noe Rebel were therein sustained which made a

greate nombre of glad hartis that dyd as they were bydden.

Carts with carriage entered ye Cittye This done, about three of the clock afternoone cam in all the carts with carriage and munition att the seide Westwick gate.

The pollicy of ye Rebellis to destroy their enemies And when the Rebellis parcevid them thus entryd the Cittye, and hoping, because the straungers knew not the streets, to assemble in Companies in many lanes where they thought by little and little they might cutt of theyr enemies. And for this purpose assemblid a greate Company in a brawde place next Christ Church callyd Tomblonde and soe devydid **The division of ye Rebellis** themselvis in iij Companies to goe on three streets to theyr enemies ward, that is one part went uppon St. Michael's streete, another on Middle Wymer streete, the third on St. Symond's and St. Peter Howngate streete by the Elme and about the Hyll next the corner late the Black Fryers shewid themselvis in battell array where they kylled iij or iiij Gentyllmen that wantid rescue. This noysid in the Market place came downe by St. John's **They assemble to ye first battel in St. Andrew's streete begun** streete and along this middle streete the wholle power in array where neere St. Andrew's on both parts were shot a greate nombre of arrows, but whyle they were shooting came Captaine Drury with his band of Hagabushes and dischargid on such a sudden that the seid Rebellis recoylid

The Rebellis recoile   whereat they were soe hastily pur-
att which were slaine   suid that many of them were feine
a C the rest were driven out   to take church yards and hyd
them under the wallis and fell flatt in the allies, which understandid, they were all slaine to the nombre of a C or there
abowt. The rest, both through the waye and Christ Church,
were soe pursuid that they fled to their Camp and soe within
one half hower were all driven out of the Cyttie where im-
The ways and streetes   mediatly were all wayes & streights
stopt & kept   kept & ramperd up except the one only Common way out of Bishops gates and there was the Ordenance
& carriage of munition as prest to goe to Mushold which
The Lord's Ordnance   when the Rebellis on the hyll saw
brought heere by the   and parcevid, then without shot or
Rebellis is taken &   powder to defend themselvis in theyr
part recovered by   Campe, and that the same had but a
Captin Drury & his men   few Welchmen to defend it &
that the King's power was busied in other placis of the Cittye where breaches was, the seid Rebellis uppon a desperate
mynde, mad a desperate enterpryse and coming from the
hyll entred uppon the seid Ordinance and other munition in
divers carts* laden with soe much powder that with two of
The Rebellis with   the greatest peices they shot into the
the seid Ordinance did   Cittye from that xxiijth day night
much hurt in ye Cittye   of August untill the end that they

were dispersid on the xxvjth day after, and therewith did shoote downe a Tower of the same gate callyd Bishops gate which slew many men that there . . . . . gardid, but the losse had bin the greater but that Capten Drury with his band recoverid part, notwithstanding hee had grett losse of men. But after theyr repulse the Lord Leiuetenant wardid the breach more strongly and kept ye Rebellis owte all that

The Lord Willowby appointed to ye place & Lord Lieuetenant & ye Marquis lodgid att Mr Steward's nyghte and appoynted the Lord Willowby with others to ward that streete & gate callyd Bishops gate and after things wel was with the Lord Marquis and others lodged att Mr Steward's howse where, after a cawdell drinking for a quarter of an hower, returnd agen to apoynt the watch till x of the clocke that hee had rest. And about this tyme the Rebellis

The Rebellis enter att Conforth & sett fire on ye howses attryed to enter about Conforth and certeyne coming over the water did set dyvers howses in South Confort on fire where was burnid a whole parish or two on both sides the way with much corne & marchantryes & stuffs and would have gon further had they not bin expulsid, for they ment to burne the whole Cittye. Notwithstanding the fire

The cause of not quenching ye fire was suffrid to burne to the end for that it was suspected that their only firing thereof was to bring ye Company to quench it whylst they,

39

the Rebellis, might attempt the like in another place or ells enter to doe further mischeefe.

The next daye Sundaye in ye morning went every one to armour, when though for the largenes of the Citty and difficilitie thereof the Lord Leiuetenant was by ye best advisid to depart til furder puissance, yeat valiantly answerid **The valiant answer** by God's grace not to depart the Cittye **of ye Lord of Warwick** but would deliver it or leave his life and notwithstanding, where least was thought, began **Another entrance** dyvers Rebellis to enter the Cittye in **of ye Rebellis** the furdest parte whoe were cum as far as the bridges, wherefore the bridge callyd the Whyt Fryars bridge was broken clene up & soe had the rest had not bin **The Rebellis** reasonable cawse shewid, but in there repuls **repulsed & slaine** was many slaine & where the gates were burnid was defendid with men. After this, because many **Souldiours appointed** soldiours had not bin lodgid nor **to howses & takered** housid a good space, was every man's howse appoynted to receive a Company; the better to make them harty went many to theyr beds and had victuals furnished which encouragid them much and then did every man take furth his stuffe and other things before hydden in placis to defend fier to minister the nedis of theis men. And now for that the Lord Leiuetenant had taken up Mr Awsten Steward's howse and sett his arms on the gate, did other

40

The taken up of   Lords, Squires and Gentlemen the like
howses for Noblemen   and for the tyme tooke each man's
howse as there owne till theyr departure when then for joye
of the victory every man set up the ragged staffe uppon
theyr gates & doors in the Lord Leiutenant's honour which
soe continued many years after and soe savely continuid that
daye. The next day being Monday the xxvjth of August, the
Lord Leiuetenant at dinner, cam about x or xi hundred
The coming of   Lance Knights* which, after they had dis-
LanceKnights   chargid their peeces to shew theyr cominge,
were allsoe lodgid in divers howses with many of their wives
that came with them.
The devyce of the   Whylst theis things were a doeing was
Rebellis for victory   devizing in the Rebellis Campe what
were best to doe for victory, and as they had oft giving
themselvis from good admonicion to theyr owne wills, soe
now, neere unto such tyme as theyr destruction was present,
had God suffrid them to bee deludid for now instead of put-
Their trust in feined   ting theyr trust in God they trustid
prophecys caused them   uppon faynid prophecies which
to be overthrown   were phantastically devisid, which prophecys they had often cawsid before to bee openly proc-
laimid in the markit & other placis as matters of greate tryall
as they thought to maintaine them, emongs which was one
that spake of such assemblys and that in Dussens Dale* there

41

should the perish both greate & small which in them that after fell owt, but theyr construct was that there they should winne the battell of ther enemies and put them to flight.

To Dussens Dale Whereuppon they fully determinyd re-
the Rebellis removid movyd all that night all ther ordin-
in hope by their prophecie ance & munition and all other
to prevaile & what they did things clene from that place
they were in before, and had devysid trenches & stakes wherein they and theyrs were intrenchid & set up greate Bulwarks of defence before & abowte and placid their or-dinance all abowt them and that the Gentylmen the prysners
How they ordrid shuld not escape they take them owte of
ye Gent. prisners theyr prysons in Surry Place and carrid them to the seid Dussens Dale with them, which was not past a myle of and somewhat more, whome to bee their defence they chained together & set them in theyr forward, whereof my Lord Lieuetenant, having intelligence by ye watch in Christ Church steeple, preparid himself to give battell and
The Lord Warwick on Teusday the xxvijth daye with his
preparid his Army powre preparid in battell arraye out
to them of his clemency att the gates callyd Gosny gates marchid to them, and notwithstanding all things prest soe saving the Gentylmen with them sent Sir Edward Knyvett* with others to see if they would yeelde, but of theyr obstin-acy would not & to begin shot of their ordenance by their

The beginning of the Battell where the Rebellis killed ye horse of the standerd Cheife Gunner, one Mules, and killed the horse of the standard bearer & hurt him in the legge, whereuppon the army shot att them & breake theyr **There array broke,** carrage and savid many of those Knights, Squires & Gentylmen which the Rebellis had cheand **Ket fled & his horse tirid at Swannington** in theyr forward as they were com-mandid to doe, when Kett, before they joynd*, with v or vi Rebellis fled & att Swannington, where his horse was tirid & hee forcid to take a barne where was a cart with corne unlading, was browt to the howse of one Mr Riches of that towne a v mile from Norwich who, though hee was left with a childe in the howse vij or viij years old, had not the spirit to depart whyles Mrs Riches was fetched from church, whome though shee rated for his demeanour, yeat did hee pray hir of contentation & to have meate; when [i.e. then] ye next morning, about iiij of ye clock, hee was browte to the Lord Leiuetenant's lodging with such as were sent for him in this ceason. The Rebellis, **What ye Rebellis did missing their Captains & how many were slaine** myssing theyr Captin Kett, as God pleasid their harts fainted they being dispercid, slayne* and a numbre greate taken prisners and put ......
churches till the next day that they cam ......
Thende of the the battell endid about 4 of ye clocke ......

43

Battel and made good peniworth thereof in ye Cittye…
of ye spoile of the array had many souldiers……
The clemency of to savely deliver them in the ……
my Lord to them many Gentlemen slayne emongs……
hee understood to bee the next day Kette ……
there against theyr will cawsing the namis of ……
How many choyse of there ……
were condemned whereof the ……
The burial of which soe did ……
ye corses deade them we ……
How ye Rebellis corses……
were hangid in ye to the……
Cross of the Markit but……
How ye Lord Warwick who……
with his Lords gave
thanks to God in *desiderantur nonnulla*
St. Peter's Church *[several lines are missing]*
How hee his……

44

Notes

So much has already been written about Kett's rebellion that full annotation of the text seemed unnecessary, and indeed impractical, in this small volume. The following notes are directed chiefly to pointing out the differences between Sotherton's account and that published in 1575 by Alexander Neville, secretary to Archbishop Matthew Parker. Quotations are from the English translation of Neville's work entitled 'Norfolk's Furies or a View of Kett's Camp'.

p. 3 'enclosing of divers common grounds' — Neville also links the rebellion closely to the loss of common land by enclosures. He also mentions the Enclosure Commission of 1549 which operated in some areas and not in others. In fact enclosure was only one symptom of what poorer farmers saw as a systematic exploitation of the law to benefit the gentry at their expense.

p. 3 'vi daie of June' — This is unquestionably an error either in the original or on the part of the copyist. The same mistake occurs on p. 6. The Wymondham Game took place annually on the Feast of St. Thomas a Becket and on the preceding day, July 6-7th.

p. 4 'Robert Kett alias Knight' — This title dates from 1395 when Robert Kett's great-grandfather, Richard, was born out of wedlock. All his male descendants bore the name 'Kett alias Knight'.

p. 4 'Flowerdew's Close' — Possibly 'Bromeclose' in Wymondham which was held by John Flowerdew. Neville gives further details of the meeting between Flowerdew and the rebels. He also quotes a reported speech by Kett to the rebels, presumably based on hearsay evidence.

p. 5 'Mount Surry' — Originally St. Leonard's Benedictine Priory, the buildings had been procured for the Earl of Surrey at the Dissolution by his father the Duke of Norfolk. It remained Kett's headquarters until the rebels left the Heath. Neville says they 'left all possible marks of their villainies in that once stately house'. He gives the number of rebels at this stage as 2,600 'vile Rabble, the Scum and Dregs of Norfolk and Suffolk'.

p. 7 'the Inglish tongue' — The full English service was introduced by the first Edwardian Act of Uniformity of January 1549, the legal date for using the new prayer book being June 9th. Its use in these circumstances so soon after the passing of the Act suggests that in practice the adoption of the English service may have preceded its legalisation. The reference also suggests that Sotherton's account was not written during Mary's reign when the Latin mass returned and the English prayer book was banned.

p. 8 'commanding precepts' — Neville gives the exact wording of 'writs' issued by Kett and reluctantly authorised by Codd, Aldrich and Watson. They begin, 'We the

King's Friends and Delegates give Authority…' and end, '…so as no violence or Injury be done to any honest or poor Man.'

p. 9 'xx thousand persons' — Neville gives 16,000 for this stage of the rebellion.

p. 9 'the Governours' — Presumably Sotherton is here referring to Kett, Codd, Aldrich and Watson. Kett also appointed from his followers two 'governors' for each of the Hundreds represented at the camp. Their names head the surviving copy of Kett's 49 demands. Neville says of the Oak of Reformation that they 'laid Baulks across and made a Roof with Boards'.

p. 12 'other places and shires in Inglond' — This is the only suggestion that men from beyond Norfolk and Suffolk joined the camp, though there may have been some attempts to raise support in Essex. The churchwardens' accounts of North Elmham offer an interesting example of participation by a contingent which was supported and financed by the parish. It included the parish constable and does not bear out the consistent down-grading of the social status of the rebels by both Sotherton and Neville.

p. 12 'jd a quarter veri good' — Neville gives the same figures for the cattle and sheep devoured by the rebels. The country west of Norwich was said to be utterly 'spoiled both of malt, beef and muttons' when Warwick

47

arrived with his army.

p. 13 'noe Gentyllmenne shuld escape' — At this point in the narrative Neville inserts a story about Matthew Parker who preached at St. Clement's, Norwich, during the rebellion. Some of the rebels evidently disliked his sermon and seized him afterwards to rob him of his 'three or four geldings'. Neville claims that he tricked them by getting a smith to rub their hooves with green copperas to make them appear tired and useless.

p. 14 'had not offended' — This was the position consistently maintained by the rebels, that they were loyal subjects of the King making justifiable complaint against the gentry and royal officials who had perverted the laws.

p. 15 'the Rebels entrid' — The seven lines preceding this phrase were clearly difficult to read, for the copyist had written several times in the margin 'fortasse legendum', meaning 'probably to be read'.

p. 14 'vj small peeces' — Neville says 'ten great peeces'.

p. 19 'Crosse of the market' — This then stood in the centre of the market place and is clearly shown on a map of 1541 (see p. 44). A more detailed drawing in 1732 by Sheldrake shows that the rood on top had been removed and some embellishments added.

p. 19 'Leonard and his brethren' — If, as is usually thought, Leonard was the son of Nicholas Sotherton senior

(Mayor of Norwich 1539) then his brothers were Thomas (Sheriff of Norwich with Leonard in 1556) and Nicholas, probably the author of this work. This would mean he was in Norwich during the rebellion, but his account does not read like that of an eye-witness.

p. 20 'William Brampton Gent.' — In the depositions against John Walker of Griston, who was hanged for his part in a riot in 1540, he is said to have intended to attack Mr Southwell (Woodrising), Mr Gray (Merton), Mr Hogan (Dunham), Mr Brampton (?) and Sir Roger Townshend (Raynham). This may be the same Mr Brampton.

p. 20 'did send abroade' — Attempts were made to get support from Lynn, and Nicholas Byron was sent with 100 men to subdue Yarmouth and obtain provisions and horses. They were refused admission, but managed to get six guns from Yarmouth's old rival, Lowestoft. They attacked Yarmouth, but were defeated and lost the guns.

p. 22 'Marquis of Northampton' — Brother to Katherine Parr, appointed Lord Lieutenant of Norfolk, July 1549.

p. 22 'Waydsworth' -- Probably intended for Wentworth. He is called Weinford on p. 26.

p. 26 'the day spring' — Neville says there was a skirmish on this night in which 300 were killed.

p. 27 'forty persons' — Neville says 140 were killed and many wounded.

p. 29 'fier that daie' — Neville says rain delayed the fires.

p. 32 'Barthylmewe Even' — St. Bartholomew's eve is actually August 23rd.

p. 34 'Hyll neere the Campe' — This may be a reference to what is now called Gas Hill where stood the ruins of St. Michael's chapel, later known as Kett's Castle.

p. 38 'C or there abowte' — Neville says that 300 were killed in this battle at St. Andrew's plain.

p. 38 'divers carts' — Neville's account of this incident in his first edition of 1575 was so disparaging to the Welsh, whom he described as 'cowardly' and 'like sheep' that it caused an outcry and was omitted from later editions.

p. 41 'Lance Knights' — Swiss Landsknechts.

p. 41 'Dussin's Dale' — Neville gives the old rhymes in English. There is little in Sotherton to assist in locating Dussindale. Anne Carter's recent discovery of 'Dussing's Deale' on a map of 1718 just to the east of Gargytt Hills in Postwick seems convincing (Norf. Arch. XXXIX pt.1) though it does not explain why the indictment of Kett says it was 'in the parishes of Thorpe and Sprowston'.

p. 42 'Sir Edward Knyvett' — Neville also mentions Thomas Palmer, a soldier of fortune serving Warwick.

p. 43 'before they joynd' — Neville does not suggest that Kett left the field before the battle began.

p. 43 'slayne' — Neville says 3,500 were killed.